# NETWORKING ON STEROIDS™

A Guide to Professional Success
via Practical Networking Tips

# A Guide to Professional Success via Practical Networking Tips

## Cathy Weaver

networking, selling, sales, business, branding, professionalism, marketing, training,
speed networking, sales training, opportunity, networking events, expos, success,
career, value proposition, identity, productivity, referral, prospects, clients, one-on-
one, follow-up, entrepreneur, business development

*Dedicated to all of us who choose to take a step or two*

*outside our comfort zones each day!*

# Contents

# What is Networking?

*Welcome to the Networking Arena! Whether you are starting your own business, working for a new company or serving as marketing director for your current company, I trust you will find some of the tips and experiences in the following pages helpful as you climb the ranks to networking expert.*

*Each of us wants to be an expert or a "go-to" person. After reading this book, my hope is that YOU will be that very person in your community!*

*~Cathy Weaver*

By its definition, **"networking"** is sometimes referred to as:

"A socioeconomic activity by which groups of like-minded businesspeople recognize, create or act upon business opportunities."

In my terms, it's a chance to make new connections and acquaintances, and to build new and lasting relationships. You will notice that neither definition of "networking" says this is a time to pass out or collect business cards or to sell actual product!

Years ago, the question was "Do you belong to any networking groups?" Today the question is "How many networking groups do you belong to?"

The way to market one's business has certainly been enhanced by all the networking that happens now. So, the questions "Where do I

go for networking?" and "How do I network effectively?" need to be answered.

Here are several points to ponder when undergoing the possibility of attending that first or hundredth networking event:

✓ It's not   netDRINKING
    or    netEATING
    or    netSITTING,
    it's    netWORKING!

✓ Do I have a plan?

✓ Who do I want to meet at this event?

✓ Did I bring enough cards?

✓ Do I bring a door prize?

# Where are Your Pom-Poms?

Is today a good day to go to that networking meeting? You need to feel your best and look your best because otherwise, you may do more harm than good for your company.

If you are not ON, you could be doing a disservice to yourself and the other guests and perhaps have the opposite effect you are attempting.

Do you have trouble getting up and getting started for the day? Is motivation one of the things that appealed to you initially about the at-home business model; but, you find yourself stuck in your PJ's for hours and you end up taking your shower around 1 p.m.? You can be your own best cheerleader and your own best motivator. We really can't rely on others to get us up and going each day.

One thing I have found helpful is to get a set of pom-poms, even at a toy or party supply store, and put them near the bathroom mirror or the dressing table or wherever you go each morning to get dressed. It's important to get motivated and off to a great start every day. We are our own best cheerleaders and sometimes we need a tangible reminder of that fact!

Put your best self forward for each event and always remember: You never get a second chance to make that first impression.

And please know, all you have to do is SMILE! It amazes me that I see so many "Gloomy Gusses" at meetings. You can tell they are having a bad day; a bad client experience; trouble at home... Oh my goodness, this would have been a GOOD day to forego that networking agenda.

YOU ARE A ROCKSTAR!

# Practice Saying "Thank You!"

Think about the last time you paid someone a compliment and their first reaction was "Oh, this old thing," or "Oh my goodness, I look so horrible today," or "I got this 100 years ago at a thrift store." Why do we struggle so much with accepting people being nice to us?

Think about the effort it took for you to say, "You look nice today," "I love your sweater" or "Your necklace is fabulous," and then the person receiving these comments responds with "Yuk!" So how did that make you feel? When someone says something nice about your appearance or your talents or your presentation, say "Thank you." It's that simple to make someone else feel good, accepted and perhaps even sincerely flattered.

> "People often say that motivation doesn't last. Well, neither does bathing; that's why we recommend it daily."
> ~ Zig Ziglar

Each event may be different: the organizer, the location and even the dress code may be different. An "After Hours" often draws a different crowd than a meeting during actual business hours, so dress accordingly. What do you wear when going to meet someone for a one-on-one appointment?

**Appearance truly does matter, regardless of the event.**

We have read and studied various wardrobe and style and business etiquette books and other articles on this topic, so we won't elaborate further here. Please note they are certainly available if these are areas in which you have further interest or even your own set of challenges.

"Bring the best of your authentic self to every opportunity."
~ John Jantsch

# First Step: Supplies

## Do you always wear a great name badge?

... perhaps with your fabulous logo on it, and do you always wear your badge on the right side of your suit? We shake hands with our right hands and our identifier goes on that right side. Name and face recognition is certainly easier when the badges are consistently worn on the right. I can walk into a room of professionals and instantly tell the true networkers. Yes, there are two schools of thought on this subject, but this one has proved consistent for me.

## So, what is on your name badge?

Yes, your name and your company name appears but what else? If the print is too small to read, that is not as effective to those meeting you for the first time, or even the tenth time. Do you want your logo to be the first thing they see or your name? It really depends on you and your company; in other words, if you have worked several places, people most likely know you, and they will find out where you work secondly. If your company brand is the identifier here, then that logo can be more predominant on your badge. Whichever way you want to be known, an expertly created name badge will do the trick.

## Have you ever been handed a business card that truly perplexes you? Ask yourself "Why?"

- How is the quality?

- Is it current, or have they "corrected" something on it?

- Can you read the name? Is there a name on it?!

- Is it clear what this person does, or does it make you want to know more about what they do?

- Does the logo look professional?

Your name badge, your appearance, your business card: EVERYTHING about that first meeting does matter!

I have actually been handed a business card that had white-out on it, as well as a hand-written phone number and email address…

This would have been the perfect time to not attend, get to a printer immediately and get some business cards that are worthy of the recipient!

# What difference does a business card really make?

I have been told by business coaches that having one's photograph on a business card is important, especially if you are new to your business or to the networking arena. The odds of having your card "filed away" in the trash can are less when you have a picture on it than when you don't. If you can't handle your photo on a card, then by all means, make sure your logo is awesome; this is another conversation starter.   You give the recipient a perfect chance to say  "Great logo!", "Great card!", "Great picture!"… something to get the ball rolling!

That professional photo is most important. There are many photographers out there who like to do location shots. You can have your professional photo taken at your office, your home, at a favorite place; wherever means the most to you so when the photo is mentioned in a networking setting, that can be your conversation starter. This is another time that hiring a professional to do your profile/business photo can make a world of difference in how you come across to the general public and to that next prospect or client.

## How much information do you want on the card?

## Is the back of your business card blank?

## Is your business card too full of information, or is there not enough information?

*There are many factors that determine a great business card but if you remember that wasted space is empty real estate but too much information is just over-whelming, you will find the perfect balance for your new prospect.*

I have seen jobseekers who have placed a mini resume on the back of their contact card. This is a great idea if their purpose for networking is to land their next job. A list of what you do or what you have done may seal the deal for that prospective employer. For business owners, having a list of what you offer can also be a great idea for the back of that business card. A printing company, for example, may wish to put: copies, faxes, name badges, plaques and awards. The possibilities here are truly endless to make that card effective without appearing cluttered.

**What happens if you win a door prize or give one, and there is no name on the card?**

Wow! Who won? Who gave this prize? Again, once you think in these terms, it will help you determine exactly what you want your card to say about you and your company, and how much information you want to include that will create just enough curiosity to precipitate that follow-up phone call.

If promotional products and logo design are not your areas of expertise, hire that perfect person. We can't all be wonderful at everything, so this would be a great first step in surrounding yourself with experts. There are many websites with free products, but their poor quality may not be what you want your potential client to first notice about you.

# Practice Makes Perfect

Every one of us who networks needs to have perfected the ever-popular and always in-demand infomercial. Whether your group offers you enough time for your name, business name and tagline or signature statement OR a thirty-second infomercial OR a sixty-second infomercial OR a two-minute explanation of your company and what you do there, the best news of all…we can practice and change the contents as the groups warrant, *emphasis* on the word ***PRACTICE!***

Never hesitate to have a trusted friend or co-worker listen to your infomercial a time or two. This small snippet in time will forever be etched in history if you make this your dynamic introduction of yourself and your company. Consider how many times a theater demands a dress rehearsal before the curtain call; your practicing of your infomercial *is* your dress rehearsal.

**The first thing I realized is that I must write down what I want to say with each version I am allowed.**

If I know I will be attending a group that offers just the first choice, above, then that one is easy. If the group I will be attending offers the other choices, I must use my time effectively to instill curiosity to make sure the other attendees will want to learn more about what I have to offer. Again, I have written down each version, so when presented with a chance for more time, I am prepared.

Henry David Thoreau said, "Do not hire a man who does your work for money, but him who does it for love of it."

*I have great news: Sometimes the best signature statements come from friends or other networkers. They hear what we are saying and sometimes they say it better or more concisely. I love learning from others, so if someone is willing to help you with your tagline, by all means, go for it!*

Of course, you know your name and you know your company name, but what is your tag line, or your "signature statement?" Sometimes people come up with rhymes to get their point across; well-received generally but the effectiveness is perhaps questionable. Not to say catchy slogans from years past still resonate in our heads and when heard again, we always know what product it is, but to the networking population today,

**...the signature statement needs to be the "hook" that prompts more questions or appointments at the end of the event.**

**What will people remember about you with only a minute or two to get to know you?**

Would you like their memory to be of your clothing, jewelry, name badge, haircut, business card or your networking card?

How effective were you today in all of your groups?

How many more friendships and relationships were formed during these opportunities?

What will your follow-up be with each of the people you met at all of these networking events this week?

Every networking "how to" offers a huge section on follow-up. *The fortune is in the follow-up, some say.* If you come home with that inevitable stack of business cards, what is your next step? Some scan the cards into their phones; others keep a large notebook; some actually call these new prospects and set up that all important one-on-one appointment. This is where we get to know more about each other: how long have you been in this business; what do you like most/least about it; who is a good referral for you; do I know anyone that you would like to meet (one of my social media connections).

Some people choose to "friend" those they have met in person on those social media sites, while others actually use that new stack of "friends" as their updated email list!

**Be careful here: If someone has not asked to be on your list for your newsletter or other promotion of your company, do not assume they want to be.**

We must always be respectful as to how we use the information we have collected from these new acquaintances, and the last thing we want to do is annoy anyone. There are great ways to follow up and the list of possibilities here is endless. Whatever you choose as your follow-up method, just be sure to do it.

"Position yourself as a center of influence - the one who knows the movers and shakers. People will respond to that, and you'll soon become what you project."
~ Bob Burg

# Timing is Everything

If your group meets monthly, you have very different responsibilities to make that group work for you than you have with a weekly group. A networking group that only meets once every thirty days gives you about twenty-five chances to schedule those all-important one-on-one interviews to get to know just one member of that group a bit better, to learn more about their business, and to ask who a good referral for them might be.

A weekly group gives you the chance to see and be seen once every seven days, so depending upon your infomercial, you will instill curiosity about your business into each attendee. The once-a-week group gives you the opportunity for a luncheon or maybe an invitation to an "after hours" with one or two of those members.

**Any get-together appointments you can schedule with your new contacts gives everyone a better chance to get to know each other, make effective connections and build those all-important relationships.**

"It's all about people. It's about networking and being nice to people and not burning any bridges."
~ Mike Davidson

## Be sure to get to each event early and even offer to be a greeter!

Being a greeter at an event is a wonderful way to get to meet everyone! You are instantly perceived as the person "in the know", the "go to" person. The leaders of the group will remember you as that special someone who sincerely wants to help and get involved. Some groups even offer special recognition and introduction during the meeting, thus getting your name and your company name 'out there' one more time.

PowerChics™ Luncheon at the Kansas City Cafe. Guess what? I signed up to be a greeter!

Always remember to meet and introduce yourself to the most important person or persons in the room: *the servers!*

We certainly don't give to get necessarily, but trust me, I know the name of every server I ever deal with whether it be at a Board meeting for ten of us or a network meeting with upwards of one hundred. When I am the speaker, I always say "Let us thank our very attentive Christina (Nicholas, Paula or whomever) for their fantastic service to us today." I am telling you the truth: That person has now become one of my greatest friends. Perhaps they are the ones to never get noticed and certainly not applauded. Next time I am in that location, do you think for one minute my cup does not runneth over? It didn't hurt for one second to give them thanks for doing a great job, and it has truly made their day much better.

## Exit Greeter: The perfect 'post' at your Networking event!

- To say Good-bye to your guests and members.

- To thank them for coming!

- To offer to Connect them with someone they did not get the chance to meet at the event...

- To meet for coffee in the next week or so, to learn more about their company and what they do there

- To invite them to your NEXT event!

# Go COIN Collecting!

*Do you want to meet the movers and shakers in the group itself? I recommend that you go COIN collecting! I give gold coins (filled with chocolate) to those who attend my seminars. This is a reminder to find out who the Centers Of Influence Networkers really are in any given organization. Every group has its own influential members, including the Board Members possibly, and each of those people could introduce you to that next prospect or client for your company.*

*People love to help others connect, so just ask! Perhaps you will become that very important "connector" in your networking arena. The more people you meet and really get to know, the easier it will become for you to become the connector, thus adding value to your networking existence.*

"Your power is almost directly proportional to the thickness of your Rolodex, and the time you spend maintaining it. Put bluntly the most potent people I've known have been the best networkers - they "know everybody from everywhere" and have just been out to lunch with most of them."

~ Tom Peters

# A Matter of Formality

Sometimes you know when you walk into a group of people if it's going to be a good fit for you and if you will eventually join. Some groups that have been around for years have very strict and written-out guidelines which are adhered to… period. Others are much more laid back and informal. Sometimes it depends on the type of business you have; sometimes it depends upon the type of person you are, but rest assured, there is a group out there for everyone. You will learn quickly that even "after hours" events are different and appeal to a variety of tastes.

For example, I have attended after-hours events where there is barely a sober person left in the joint, and I have attended black tie after hours events with upwards of nine hundred people where the food was served on trays by perfectly attired wait staff. Make sure you research where you are going and always have a plan, even for these events. You may have a chance to look, via the internet, at the attendee list prior to showing up. That is a bonus, to be sure. Use that information to your extreme advantage and if there is a VIP who will be attending, do a little

info check on that person, then you can be quite the conversationalist if you get to meet him or her in person.

It is the funniest thing to me that someone who relies mostly on networking to market themselves and/or their business that they do not carry business cards with them at all times! *You simply never know when you will meet someone, strike up that conversation and both of you realize that they need your product or service and you do not have a business card with you.* What is wrong with that picture?

Whether your group is strict or not, or whether you are attending a meeting during business hours or after business hours, be sure you are prepared to talk business if the need presents itself. Too much to eat or drink is never a great idea, and when you are out, be sure to have a way for people to contact you. Once everyone gets home or back to the office, without that contact information, it will be difficult to follow up.

"More business decisions occur over lunch and dinner than at any other time, yet no MBA courses are given on the subject."
~ Peter Drucker

# How 'Bout Some Bling?

## Balloon Garden

*Carol Miner*
***balloongarden.com***

Sometimes I hear from business owners that they are just too shy to go out and personally market their business. They can do the internet marketing, but in-person marketing? No way. I tell them they just need a good opener!

### What is your conversation starter?

There are actually several things you can do to start a conversation. For me, I sometimes will wear a balloon corsage, a silk flower or flashy jewelry. This needs to be incorporated into what will eventually be your signature "look," but for the meantime, it will be your way to start, or break into, a conversation with those you don't know well, or have not ever met before.

I have included a photo of one of the balloon corsages I have worn. These are provided for me by a lady I met while networking, Carol Miner of ***Balloon Garden*** (www.balloongarden.com). Carol has supplied me with all types of corsages: green for St. Patrick's Day and the entire month of March; red with hearts not only for Valentine's Day but because February is *"Go Red For Women"* (women's heart-health month); and a variety of others.

The great news is since they are balloons and not real flowers, they last forever. Every time I wear one, someone always says, "That is very pretty," to which I always respond, "Thank you so much, I love it. A dear friend made it for me and it is actually made from balloons!" Guess what? I just had my corsage get that conversation started and Carol may end up with a new client. A true win/win for all of us was initiated by my wearing of that well-chosen accessory piece.

Now that you have started the conversation with your flower, pin or name badge, what will you say next?

A great networker will always say, "Tell me something about you." That person can now decide what he or she wants you to know about them.

Other great conversation starters:

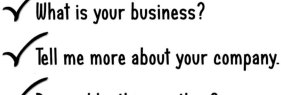 What is your business?

✓ Tell me more about your company.

✓ Do you like this weather?

✓ Have you always lived in Kansas City?

✓ Do you drink coffee?

✓ Do you have any pets?

*People love to talk about themselves – you just need to ask the right questions to get the ball rolling.*

## What happens when the conversation continues for much longer than you wanted?

If after a couple of your questions, the other person has not flipped the conversation back to you, you will know you are not communicating with a pro. There should be a great exchange of thoughts going between you and him or her by now, and if that has not happened, you may need to determine if this person will be a great source of referrals for you, a prospect for your product or merely a networking acquaintance.

None of the above is a good or bad thing – it is just the category into which they must be placed. If you had a goal to meet and get to know three to five people at this event and this person so far knows nothing about you, it may be time to move on to the next person. I have a few ways to get away from your current contact and move on to another person in the upcoming chapters. Stay tuned!

"Take action every day. It doesn't have to be dramatic action, but every day, stick with it. Spend time on things that make you proud, that stretch and strengthen you."
~ Phillip Humbert

# Don't Get too Comfy

**Exercise for the day:**

*In my seminars, one of the first things I do is ask everyone in the room if they are ready for some calisthenics, to which most reply "No," especially after a full luncheon or dinner. C'mon now, it won't be that bad. You can do this one from your sitting position in your chairs.*

*Hold your arms up – cross them – look down to see which arm is over which. Now repeat this procedure but, this time, fold your arms with the opposite arm on top. Not too easy, is it?*

This exercise reminds us that every time we or someone else crosses their arms that we need to step outside the box and do something each day that is truly a challenge or a struggle; albeit a rather small one.

# Get out of your comfort zone and do something a bit uncomfortable each day!

It is so easy and comfortable to always sit with people you already know. That will not help you with your "plan" for today to make new connections and find new clients. So you can stand near the food or drink table and discuss the menu, the drink options, the name badge, the flower or the venue. There are so many ways to start conversations, keeping in mind this is not a time to sell your product or service. If being the first one to speak is outside your comfort zone, you just succeeded for the day! This is not a time to collect or distribute tons of business cards but to find out more about the person standing near you. If the conversation is generic, you will never come off as "pushy."

# Did You Win?

**If your event offers door prizes, then bring one!**

These items are very often overlooked and underrated. If your company has items that you can give away, be sure they are current, or items that have not expired. I once received a packet of a person's products in which each of the items had dates on them and they were old. Do you think for one second that I would have used them? No, nor would I have called to see if I could get more! The entire point of the door prize had been negated. That company would never be one that I would recommend if this is the caliber of person they have allowed to sell their line.

Let's say you have a cosmetic company and you are offering lip gloss, hand cream or sunscreen as your door prize. Put that item in a fancy sack or basket clearly marked with your name via business

"Recognize that giveaway items serve as silent ambassadors, reinforcing your Expert Identity - choose them carefully!"

~ Susan Friedman

card and always include a catalog with your current products. Now comes the follow-up part. Be sure to watch who wins your fabulous basket of goodies.

You automatically have a warm lead when you call and say, "I saw you won my door prize the other day at our luncheon. Wasn't that a fun event? What is the name of your company? Do you have time next week for a one-on-one appointment? I would like to get to know more about your business and see if we could be referral partners."

In my opinion, THAT is the true purpose of taking a door prize to a networking event!

On the flip side, if you win a door prize, be sure to contact the donor if they haven't contacted you already. A couple of days is enough time for that follow-up phone call.

**Forty-eight hours should be the *maximum* time for follow-up on a door prize!**

Be sure to call and thank them. Use this opportunity to schedule that one-on-one meeting so you can decide if you would make mutually beneficial referral partners. The giver of the gift will be flattered that you took the time to call and say "Thank you." They may be very impressed that you took the initiative to get to know more about their company.

What you give says a lot about you as a business owner. What if it is not practical for you to give a gift relating to your company, such as if you are a financial advisor. In this case, a plant, a box of fancy candy or a gift card to a local finery would be appropriate; the precursor to your follow-up call to set that appointment. This is a great way to have a warm lead and not have to make a cold call to get to know more about that person or their company.

What is a bonus to giving door prizes? Your name and/or the name of your company are mentioned publicly at the event. The other bonus, the name of the recipient and their company is also mentioned. Door prizes are great ways to get publicity with very little expense. Don't overlook or underutilize the power of the door prize!

✓ Your name is announced.

✓ Your company is announced publicly.

✓ It's a chance for a follow-up appointment.

✓ The recipient's name and company are announced publicly.

✓ No need for cold calls! Bring door prizes and make great contacts with the winner.

"Creative thinking is not a talent, it is a skill that can be learnt. It empowers people by adding strength to their natural abilities which improves teamwork, productivity and where appropriate profits."
~ Edward de Bono

# Bet You Didn't Expect This...

*"The currency of real networking is not greed but generosity."*
~ Keith Ferrazzi

One of the funniest things I have noticed about human nature is people will never forget you for asking the one question, "What can I do for you?" NO ONE expects that from a networker. We all know that we attend networking events to schedule appointments and/or to create new partnerships or referral networks. Right?

Wrong! Networking events are not really times to collect business cards or to pass many of yours out; they are times to find out more about a person and what their needs really are.

Some of those get-acquainted questions could be:

✓ "How long have you been in this type of business?"

✓ "What industry were you in before this?"

✓ "Where else do you go for networking?"

✓ "What other ways do you market your business?"

Never be afraid to learn from others and never be afraid to ask questions. People love to talk about themselves, and you can get quite a conversation started with just the right set of questions.

***Who would be a good referral for you?*** If you ask that question, the person knows you sincerely want to help them build their business, and you can be the one to connect them with that all-important next client – another win/win for each of you. Back to being that connector in your community, you will be remembered as the mover and the shaker in your networking arena. It's a great feeling to put a new business relationship and partnership together, and you will be remembered for having done that.

Another conversation skill I learned at a seminar for my company is the art of controlling the conversation. This does not mean dominating the conversation; it means guiding the conversation to end up where YOU want it. If you have a product or service that can truly help people, you need to get the conversation headed toward that product or service. There are skills you can learn to help you do this.

## Try this exercise, as it works every time.

*Ask your group, or in my case, a seminar setting, "How many suits are in a deck of cards?"*

"Four," they will answer.

*"What are they?"*

"Hearts, diamonds, spades, and clubs."

*"Excellent, now of those four, pick two."*

Let's say they pick "Diamonds and spades"

*"That leaves what?*

"Hearts and clubs!" – – ⟶  *This question depends upon their answer! You are starting to "steer the conversation".*

*"Awesome. Now of the hearts and clubs, pick one."*

They respond, "Clubs!"

*"That leaves what?"* - - - - - - - - - - - - - - - - -> *If they choose*
*'Hearts' you would skip the*
"Hearts!"
*next question...*
*"Exactly…now how many face cards are there* *You're getting it...*
*in our remaining suit of hearts?*

"Three"

*"What are they?"*

"Jack, Queen, King of Hearts."

*"Now of those three, pick two."*

"Queen and Jack of Hearts"

*"Pick one."* - - - - - - - - - - - - - - - - -> *If they*
*leave out the Queen,*
"Jack." *your next question would*
*be "What's Left?"*
*"Ok, that leaves what?"*

"The Queen of Hearts!"

That is exactly the card you have in your wallet or your portfolio to show them. In my case, I have a large laminated Queen of Hearts. The audience is awestruck at the card trick but literally what I did is control which way this conversation went, one step at a time. No matter what they pick, you will decide what is left or what is the "correct" choice.

You can determine what subject you and your new friend will discuss. Again, this is not manipulation; it is effective networking. Rather than not have a plan or a point to the polite conversation, you can control where the conversation will lead: inviting that person to another event, inviting them to a one-on-one, seeing if they are pleased with their current company/product/pay scale – You determine where this conversation will go. Pretend the Queen of Hearts is anything – a dollar bill even.

## How will you get the conversation to be that of cold hard cash?

## It CAN be done!

When we ask, "What can I do for you?" we truly want to help that person, either by offering our product to them or offering other places for them to go to market their product or service.

"Try not to become a man of success, but rather try to become a man of value."
~Albert Einstein

# Check Your Schedule

You now have that perfect name badge, excellent business card, fantastic infomercial and you have attended several networking events – now you're ready for the big leagues and for that one-on-one appointment with that person with whom you said you would follow-up.  What is the procedure?

*I once spent four hours at a one-on-one. Before you flip out at the fact that I stayed anywhere for four hours, let me tell you, I truly was testing the person to see why or what would cause him to decide our time together was up.*

*Well, after incessantly chatting about everything he had done in his lifetime, never did he ask about my company, assuming he already knew what I did. Since he never asked ME any questions about any needs I may have or other specifics, he had no idea if I could use his product or service OR if I would be a good fit for his company.  Finally he got a few text messages and said he had ANOTHER one-on-one meeting with another member of our networking group and he had better get there! Wow!*

*People get so wrapped up in talking about themselves that they forget to start asking questions about you.*

"I like to define networking as cultivating mutually beneficial, give-and-take, win-win relationships... The end result may be to develop a large and diverse group of people who will gladly and continually refer a lot of business to us, while we do the same for them."

~ Bob Burg

First of all, let me just say, I have been on many one-on-one appointments – some fabulous and others less than stellar. The good news is I was able to connect with another person on the planet. The next question may be, "How effective was that meeting?"

If you are the one to call and schedule this appointment, just keep it light! Say "It was nice to meet you the other day at (Chamber X), and I wanted to know when would be a good time for us to meet for coffee." That puts the ball in the other person's court. Once the schedule and location is worked out, you are headed for that meeting.

Casual conversation ensues and you get to truly learn more about that individual. How did you get started in this business, what did you do before, what do you like about it, what do you not, and who is a good referral for you? *Again, the list of questions is huge.* This is the time that you will be able to tell if you are with a true professional. How many questions will you ask before that person flips it back to you?

I gave the example of what *not* to do during a one-on-one appointment. Now, I will let you know that a *great* one-on-one is meeting a business networker for coffee or lunch and discussing each other's business history and current businesses with a possible interjection about family or children or pets, if warranted. Then you can discuss the chance that you could be great referral partners for each other! Think about a realtor partnering with a mortgage banker or a title company, and what a perfect match that would be.

*It is so important to make these appointments and learn all you can about each other.*

**You know the rule:
People do business with others who they know, like, and trust, so you need to make sure you are one of those people.**

37

# Networking Superstar™ by WOW GRAFIX™
## TRADING CARDS

*Share your personality with potential partners and clients.*

www.wowgrafix.com | 913.538.1448

# Never Been There

You would not believe how many people look shocked when I give out my networking card with so many of my networking groups and locations listed right on it. I would like to publicly thank my great friends, who I met at a networking group a few months after I started my business, Angie and Chris O'Connor with *Writing on the Wall Grafix, Inc.* I have included a graphic of my "networking" card.

## If we are not here to support each other and help each other thrive, then why are we here?

When I first started actively networking in 2008, I had to try to find lots of groups to attend to spread the word about my product and my income opportunity. One thing lead to another, and when I lamented one time to Angie that I had to go home after a full day of networking and email all my new friends my list of groups, she inquired why I didn't just put all this information on her "Networking SuperStar™" Trading Card. Thus, my "SuperStar" networking card was born. The great news is, as my groups change, Angie changes my list with each 1000 cards printed. I believe that if each of us succeeds, the economic downturn will truly be a thing of the past.

# Guess Who Just Walked In

*Now what if the competition comes strolling into your event? What do you have to offer that the other guy does not? What is your value proposition? What makes you stand out from your competition? What can you do to be different from anyone else? How can you become a more effective networker?*

Many of us have heard this story before: A hair salon owner was thriving in his business, when across the street from his shop opened a chain that does haircuts. The owner of that chain put up a banner that read:

Now, the independent owner saw his demise in that banner. What was he going to do? He couldn't compete with $8 haircuts. ***This was the perfect opportunity for him to think outside the box!*** The next day a banner appeared over his salon:

The chain was gone and the independent
thinker was the victor.

If there are two or even ten other insurance salesmen in the room, what do you have to offer that the others do not?

In my case, I have my networking card that offers to those just starting out a list of some other groups in the area along with my company website and information about my business. This way, I can help them with my product as well as offer to help them get more groups on their list of places to go to market their own businesses. Since no one else offers what I do, my value proposition is helping others get started networking or giving seasoned veterans new groups to tackle.

The great news about having many different groups to attend is that we have groups with numbers in the tens and twenties to groups of fifty or more members. Some big groups, like various Chambers of Commerce may have two hundred or more weekly attendance with guests and members. The recipient of my card gets to choose their own comfort level, where they are right now, and progress to some of the bigger groups as their skill level increases.

# What is YOUR value proposition?

# What is YOUR comfort level?

# All the Way to the Poor House

*Robert Kiyosaki says, "The richest people in the world look for and build networks, everyone else looks for work."*

Periodically, there must be a re-evaluation of what groups have worked and what groups have not. One of my networking friends, *Mickey, the Cotton Candy Man*, refers to this as "networking yourself into the poor house." By joining so many groups, you would have to make a fortune to pay all the required membership fees.

*Realizing we only get out of something what we put into it, you do need to ask,*

"What has my being a member of this group accomplished, for me personally and certainly for my business?"

You know the saying, "You can't keep beating a dead horse," but you don't want to quit a group too soon just because you have not sold your product or service yet to any of its members. The sales process for some can certainly be a slow one; for others, usually in the service industry, it is much quicker. Have you gotten a new client, prospect or a referral for your product from this networking partnership? If not, this could be the time for a review.

The cost of each group varies; some offer social media exposure, web presence, opportunities for events and vendor expos, or motivation and encouragement. Depending upon the organizer of the group, the possibilities are truly endless.

NEW CLIENTS

PROSPECTS

REFERRALS

EXPOSURE

WEB PRESENCE

EVENTS & EXPOS

One of the first groups I joined was *KC Women's Network (KCWN)*. Candice Diddle, with *Capture KC Sports Photography*, is the leader of that group and she asked me to serve on the Board with her. We have several positions on that Board and the numbers of ladies who continue to join and prosper has been fantastic. The fee for this group is only $36 per year! High membership fees are not necessary if the group is run efficiently and effectively, and this group meets twice a month with a *Ladies Night Out* usually monthly. This offers plenty of opportunity to get to know the other members.

If you can imagine, *KCWN* also did a vendor Expo in 2011, and the fee was only $25 to be a part of that event!

Another thing you can try, if you have not felt a connection to a particular membership group, is to send a business partner, team member or someone you feel is competent and effective as a networker and see if they have different results. Sometimes it is not the group, but the chemistry with you that could be the issue. You can actually feel if a certain group is a great fit for your company and your personality, and you can totally feel if it is not.

# Cut your losses & move on to another group!

The great news is: there are numerous events in every city across this country, so you will never have a lack of places to go to market your product or service. And always remember, if there is not a group out there like you would like to have, start one yourself!

"Success - my nomination for the single most important ingredient is energy well directed."
~ Louis Lundborg

"If you want to achieve things in life, you've just got to do them, and if you're talented and smart, you'll succeed."
~ Juliana Hatfield

# Just Do It!

Recently I have been enlisted to start a [LIKE NO OTHER] Ladies Networking group that will eventually go nationwide. Where does one begin? The great news is, with all the groups I have attended over these years, I have a perfect idea of what need is not being met in the ladies networking arena. Suffice it to say, the ISP is a true deficit topic so that is the direction this group will go.

*(PS - ISP in this case, is Indulge, Support and Pamper!!! Stay Tuned!)*

The first decisions are certainly basic:

✓ Decide WHO you want at this meeting;

✓ WHAT businesses you would like represented;

✓ WHEN the group will meet;

✓ WHERE the meeting will be held;

✓ WHY there needs to be a meeting of this kind; and

✓ HOW the attendees will mutually benefit.

Hopefully, in your area there are restaurants and coffee houses which are willing to have many people come to their establishment to meet, especially if you choose a time that is not their busy time. A great venue is an enticement to attend, right off the bat. The day of the event is also important. Check around and make sure you are not conflicting with any other popular meetings such as large Chambers of Commerce, Lions Club or Rotary groups. You don't want to compete with already well-supported events.

By now in your career, you may have met the Centers of Influence Networkers (COINs), in your area. They could connect you to business people who would like to attend your new group. Remember, one of these COINs would love to be the connector for you.

There are no right or wrong answers to these questions, and the great news is: it's totally up to you!

## What will the actual agenda be?

## Will this be open networking with no formality?

Will this be a strict and formal meeting?

Are you requiring members to pass referrals to one another?

Will you charge for this event?

Will there be infomercials and non-profit announcements?

Is the first meeting free?

It sounds like lots to think about, but it comes together nicely, especially if you write down some of the key points.

When your guests arrive at the appointed location at the perfect time, they will all get a chance to meet each other. As attendees gather, this is a great opportunity for you to introduce yourself and then to introduce your guests to each other. One leads to another and pretty soon the noise level indicates success. Once the allotted open networking time is up, you may call the meeting to order, thank everyone for coming and begin with each person's infomercial.

There are so many ways to start this process: Choose a card from the basket you had at the sign in table; go around the room in order; for more established groups you may have each attendee choose a card from the basket and they must do THAT person's infomercial! Obviously, for this last choice to work, this must be with business owners who have been attending for a while. Just make sure no one is overlooked in case they did not have a card to toss in or if they were accidentally "skipped."

*Will your event have door prizes?*

*Who brought one?*

*Does it require explanation?*

*Who will choose the winner/s?*

These groups are all about making connections and building relationships, so the bottom line needs to be: ***have fun***.

If this will be your first attempt at a group, anticipate a few "oops" moments. This will be a wonderful memory as your group expands. Take a few pictures to post on your favorite social media site. It will be great to look back on your first meeting and see how your group has grown over the months or years. Make that memory!

# Your First Car?

*"Great is the human who has not lost his childlike heart."*
~ Mencius (Meng-Tse) 4th century BCE

*This is where it gets really fun.* If you have a group of brand new people to networking or just new to this group, "ice breakers" are always a great way to get the room rockin'. I have made charts with questions, each on a different color paper, cut them into squares and put a few on each table around the room; or you can let the guest select his or her question from a basket.

Some of the questions that have had great interest are:

✓ "What is something that no one knows about you?"

✓ "What was your first car?"

✓ "What high school did you attend?"

✓ "Are you a morning or night person?"

✓ "Where were you born?"

✓ "When you were younger, who was your favorite super hero?"

✓ "What is the first thing you would do if you won the lottery? "

✓ "What is your favorite flavor of ice cream?"

✓ "Where is your favorite travel destination?"

The list is truly endless and you can use the internet to help you compile these lists.

You will be amazed at how much people will remember during these sessions as opposed to the business portion of the event. If you had a super cool car in high school, especially if you still have it, the reaction in the room is almost deafening! Be creative and use this time to think "way outside that box."  The purpose of any group, hopefully, is to get to know each other better. I can refer more of my friends, family members and clients to you if I already know lots about you and if I can trust you. These exercises are great ways to accomplish both.

# Define: "Good"

**Sometimes during the infomercials, the organizer will say to add who is a "Good" referral for you.**

**This is a great chance to let the group know who you would like to meet so you could share what your company offers and how that product or service could help them.**

If you are in cosmetics, a *good* referral for you is not someone with SKIN – you need to be more specific. More likely, you need a fashion-conscious lady who is well-connected in her neighborhood and willing to host a party, so you can show the guests how your fabulous product could enhance their appearance.

What if you are a truck driver? You are not necessarily looking for someone who has product that needs hauling; you may be looking for someone who is quick and great on the computer to help you with logistics so you can avoid the dreaded "dead head" return trip home. It depends on your particular business, but it is a great chance to put the word out what is a good fit for your current need. Always be prepared for this opportunity!

As I mentioned in previous chapters, some groups are very strict while others are not so. If your group requires referrals, make sure you know this qualification: someone with whom you have already spoken. Some groups accept the warm lead approach: a person asking for a painter, a plumber, or a graphic designer. There are groups that just want to share business contact information, and the members will take it from there. Let's say you are in the water technology business, you may be looking for more than just people with faucets; be specific!

Before you put out there what you are looking for, make sure you know the difference between a cold call, a warm lead, and a referral.

A **"COLD CALL"** you can do from the phone book or the internet;

a **"WARM LEAD"** is a name from a person who has already told that person you will be calling;

and a **"REFERRAL"** is someone who may need your services – they just may not know it yet!

# Gotta Run!

## What If I Get STUCK With Someone Who Just Won't Let Go?

This happens to each of us from time to time: you attend a networking event, someone you already know approaches you, and usually due to their discomfort in these situations, this person stays with you as long as they can!

Some of the ways to break free that I have found to be effective include: "It was so great to see you again," "Excuse me as I need to meet some new prospects for my company," "Is there anyone you would like to meet that I could introduce you to?" or "Well then, I hope to see you again very soon. Have a great day!"

Some of these may seem rather harsh but you did come to this event with a plan in mind, and chatting with an acquaintance or a friend will not get your goals accomplished. Be extremely polite but this is the time you must get your point across.

"The secret of man's success resides in his insight into the moods of people, and his tact in dealing with them."
~ J. G. Holland

# Don't Try This On Me!

*Regardless of which training system you have chosen to use with your business model, each of us has used different "scripts" from time to time when prospecting for new clients.*

I received a phone call from a networking acquaintance who I had not heard from or about in a couple years. I couldn't imagine what she wanted or needed, so I took the call. After a small amount of introductory chatter, I received her script:

> *"Do you have time to watch a short video clip right now?"*
>
> "No, I won't have more time until tomorrow afternoon."
>
> *"How about I call you at 8 p.m. tomorrow night, will that give you enough time to watch it?"*
>
> "Yes, that would be fine."

Knowing full well I was being "pitched" on something, I hurried to my computer to take a look. Just as I suspected...

THE LATEST & GREATEST anti-aging pill ON THE PLANET HAD JUST BEEN DISCOVERED!

What a find! So I waited patiently till the appointed 8 p.m. the next evening and sure enough, she called promptly.

*"What did you like about what you saw?"*

I told her the clip was very well done – very professional.

*"What else did you like about what you saw?"*

"Well, it sounds like quite a breakthrough for those people who are not excited about the aging process."

*"You don't close a sale, you open a relationship if you want to build a long-term, successful enterprise." ~ Patricia Fripp*

*"Is there anything else that comes to mind about the clip?"*

"No, that is about it."

*"Cathy, I think this product and your water (I am a Kangen Water® distributor) would be a perfect fit!"*

So I responded, "Well, how fabulous. It sounds like you are ready to get your water machine!"

Much to her dismay, I turned the conversation around to HER buying MY product, since she already said it was a great fit with her pills. Her goal, of course, had been for ME to become a representative for her supplement line.

## Never try to sell a seller and always know your prospect.

She obviously didn't know that I had already used the exact same script she had tried on me, nor did she figure I would think to turn the pitch around to her buying my product. When you set appointments or schedule one-on-ones, be careful not to get in over your head.

# Warm Fuzzy

What does "Pay It Forward" have to do with networking? I have always felt that we only take with us that which we give away, so to that end, I created a business card. Here's what it looks like:

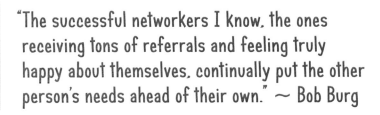

> "The successful networkers I know, the ones receiving tons of referrals and feeling truly happy about themselves, continually put the other person's needs ahead of their own." ~ Bob Burg

Say, for example, you have scheduled that one-on-one in a coffee shop. Why not give the "Pay It Forward" card to the server or the cashier, letting him or her know that you don't want to pay for a baseball team, but when someone comes in for their daily "fix," please hand them this card. When you are finished with your meeting, go to the counter and settle up, paying for the recipient's beverage or food item.

I never ask to be identified, but the stories the servers have conveyed have been priceless. One lady said that she had never won anything in her life and she felt like today she won the lottery!

**Just one more very touching story
to share with you:**

One of my networking friends asked to have ten of my "Pay It Forward" cards. She thought this would be a great way to get her out of her own funk.

# When you help others, YOU always feel better!

So I gave her ten of them. She was ecstatic one day as she called with this report:

"I wanted you to know that at a restaurant last night with a client, I gave the server one of your "Pay It Forward" cards and told her I didn't want to feed a baseball team, but if she would please select someone who may be needful or happy to receive this "gift" to please give it to them. Pretty soon every server in the place was abuzz with excitement. The selected recipient was a single mom with two young children who was treating her offspring to a dinner out. To have this paid for was like a true gift from God!"

The single mom was crying, the server was crying, and when my friend's server conveyed what had happened, she and her client were both in tears. What an impact this little card has had over the years. What were YOU able to give away today?

# Can You Help?

Once you have established yourself as someone who can really get things done and help get goals accomplished, you may be asked to help with various fundraising endeavors. Do you promote their events by physically handing out flyers or brochures? Are you able to promote their event via the social media sites? Do you work at their event? Are you willing to donate an item for their silent auction? Would you like to attend this fundraising event? There are SO many ways to help others and I am thrilled to have been able to be a part of so many of these activities.

Another way to help out is the Citizens Academy at your local Sheriff's Department or Police Department. These organizations need the help of volunteers to keep the actual staff available to do the duties to which they were assigned.

**Volunteering is a great way to stay involved & get motivated.**

Most of the public service budgets have been cut drastically, so these are areas that need volunteers more than ever!

"Stop selling. Start helping."
~ Zig Ziglar

# If You Can't Say Something Nice

If you are not familiar with **edification**, this might be a great time to learn it and to practice it. Whether you have a coach, a mentor, some well-respected friend or business partner, you may be able to practice the art of edification with any of these. When someone makes the introductions of members of the Board or the other VIP's at an event, that is the chance to practice edification.

**Edification is basically the act of uplifting another.**

This is NOT the time for idle flattery but a time to give sincere compliments and let those who are listening realize how fabulous this person is; be it the guest speaker, the host, the sponsor for the event, a business partner or team member who just achieved another milestone. Making someone's day has always been a goal of mine long before I knew the term "edification," and now I try to edify someone every day. The response to this act has had an amazing ripple effect. Practice, as always, makes perfect.

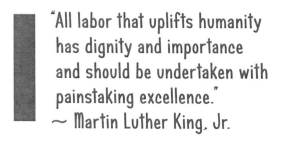

"All labor that uplifts humanity has dignity and importance and should be undertaken with painstaking excellence."
~ Martin Luther King, Jr.

"Most people think "selling" is the same as "talking". But the most effective salespeople know that listening is the most important part of their job."

~ Roy Bartell

# The Synchronized Event

*We have talked about the perfect name badge, the great logo, an awesome business card and the locations and days of the week for meetings plus the types of networking events to attend. Now, what if you are invited to a SPEED Networking event? This is a fabulous opportunity to meet MANY people in a one-on-one format very quickly.*

I will tell you the way I have conducted some of these events myself, and of course, there are many variations.

Let's say we limit this Speed Networking event to 40 attendees. We will have 4 groups with 10 people each. To make this easy to explain, we will make 10 each in the A,B,C,D group. Each letter will have time at the beginning to network amongst themselves. Perhaps this will be a luncheon meeting so each letter will be dining with others of its own letter as the event begins. Let's get started!

NOW the A's will be seated on one side of a long table and they will stay put. The B's will sit across from them and will move as instructed. At another long table, the C's will be seated and stay put for the first 2 rounds. The D's will sit across from the C's and they will move at the appointed time.

# ROUND ONE

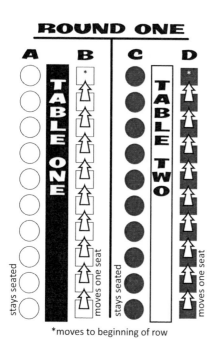

*moves to beginning of row

Depending upon the amount of time allotted for this networking event, each person will speak for let's say, one minute, then a bell will ring and the person who is seated across will do their infomercial. Can you see why rehearsing those infomercials is so important? Now the A's are speaking to the B's and the C's are speaking to the D's. When the bell rings after the sixty seconds is up, the B's will speak to the A's and the D's will speak to the C's.

# ROUND TWO

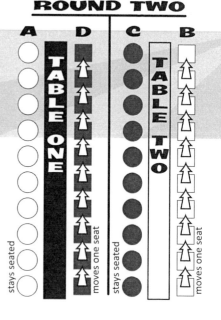

After the next one minute segment, a longer bell will be rung and this signals the time for the B's and the D's to move to the next chair in the row. Remember the A's and the C's don't move. The same one minute infomercial is now timed, a bell is rung, the other person speaks and now the longer bell signifies the moving of the B's and D's. This continues all the way, ten times, so that each A gets to speak with each B and each C gets to speak with each D.

# ROUND THREE

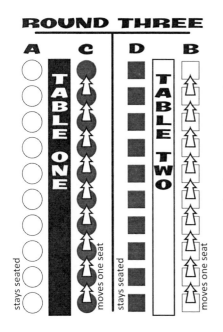

This time we move the B's to the D section and the D's move where the B's were seated. Again, the one minute timers for each infomercial follow the same process as mentioned in the previous paragraphs. After these 10 people have spoken with each of this group, the D's will now move where the C's are and the C's will move where the D's were. Now we have the A's speaking with C's and the D's and B's have a chance to meet.

As you can see, this is a very organized way to have 40 people meet each other in a very quick manner.

This is the perfect time to offer business cards, brochures, special offers, catalogs, monthly specials and a request for what type of customer or team member you may be looking for.

Yes, a minute goes by very fast but you will get your infomercial down to a minute if you practice. These minutes can be very effective once you have actually written down exactly what you want to say to be the most concise in your short amount of time.

Speed Networking events can be very fun and effective if run correctly but on the flip side, some I have attended have been like three-ring circuses. The circus version is not really conducive to recommend that follow-up phone call or email since the atmosphere in the room was less than business-like, but again what you do with this bag of business cards and brochures is certainly up to you.

Here are a few tips I have learned over the years if you are taking on the task of organizing your own Speed Networking event:

✓ Bring name badges (not everyone will have read this book). Your attendees will be more at ease if they aren't trying to remember a name instead of actively listening to the other person's infomercial.

✓ Offer pens and pads of paper so each person can take notes about the persons they meet.

✓ Make available a bag for each attendee
to keep collected items in as well as the
ones they will receive from those they
meet during each infomercial.

✓ Make the event into a great sponsorship
opportunity.

A very great networker I know is Sandy James of *Cookies by Design*™ fame. Sandy actually brings cookies with her logo on each one, wrapped in cellophane and tied with a ribbon that has her wonderful business card attached. During the infomercials, Sandy offers her 'card' to each person and a catalog featuring all of her fabulous cookie bouquets and a message that says her company delivers anywhere in the metro area. Who do you suppose was the most popular person at her Speed Networking opportunity?

Be creative and memorable and each of these types
of events will be chances for you to meet that next
perfect client or referral partner.

Depending upon the time frame, the location, the organizer and what types of businesses are involved, Speed Networking events can offer door prizes, too. We have discussed the 'purpose' of door prizes in previous chapters but suffice it to say...

If the event allows and requests door prizes, get
your name on something wonderful and donate a
door prize to that meeting!

## Now for the "Follow Up" from your Speed Networking event

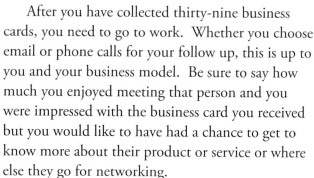

After you have collected thirty-nine business cards, you need to go to work. Whether you choose email or phone calls for your follow up, this is up to you and your business model. Be sure to say how much you enjoyed meeting that person and you were impressed with the business card you received but you would like to have had a chance to get to know more about their product or service or where else they go for networking.

This is a great time to remember that everyone loves to talk about themselves and they will certainly acknowledge the fact that you were quick to do the follow-up phone call or email message.

Will this be the time you schedule that one-on-one or will this be the time you want to sign them up for your monthly or weekly or annual e-newsletter? You decide what point you want to make with this person, especially if you think you would make great referral partners. Dare to say here that not every product or service will be a great fit for what you do, but everyone knows someone who may be able to help this other person out. Be willing to be that referral partner and you will be known as the connector in your area.

# Glean Away

Effective networkers have their own style, and if yours has yet to be established, take heart. There really is more than one way to become a great networker. This book was designed to give you some tips to make your networking time more productive, and in turn to help you with your business goals. Perhaps you have gleaned something that you can use at your daily or weekly or monthly events.

Whether you think networking is an art form or a chore, I hope this book has helped to take some of the mystique out of what you may have heard.

# Continued success to each of you & I DO hope we meet in person!